SCIENCE FAIR PROJECTS

Weather

Joel Rubin

Heinemann Library
Chicago, Illinois

Produced for Heinemann Library by White-Thomson Publishing Ltd.
Page layout by Tim Mayer and Alison Walper
Edited by Brian Fitzgerald
Photo research by Amy Sparks
Illustrations by Cavedweller Studio
Printed and bound in China by Leo Paper Group

12 11 10 09 08
10 9 8 7 6 5 4 3 2 1

Library of Congress Cataloging-in-Publication Data
Rubin, Joel.
   Weather / Joel Rubin.
      p. cm. — (Science fair projects)
   Includes bibliographical references and index.
   ISBN 978-1-4034-7912-9 (hc)
   1. Weather—Experiments—Juvenile literature. 2. Science projects—Juvenile literature.
   3. Meteorology—Juvenile literature. I. Title.
   QC981.3.R83 2007
   551.6—dc22

                                        2006039548

Acknowledgments
The author and publishers are grateful to the following for permission to reproduce copyright
material: Corbis/Daniel Aguilar/Reuters, **p. 8**; iStockphoto.com, **title page, pp. 32,** (Monte
Wilson), **6** (Panagiotis Karageorgakis), **12** (Fabio Bustamante), **20** (Shane Link), **24** (Sergey
Dubrovskiy), **28** (Volodymyr Kyrylyuk), **30tl** (Norbert - Zsolt Suto), **30tr** (Amy Walters), **30br,
36** (Andrew Penner), **39** (Jacob Carroll), **40** (Stephen Brake), **41** (Ashok Rodrigues); Masterfile/
Andrew Douglas, **p. 4**; National Oceanic and Atmospheric Administration/Department of
Commerce, **pp. 16, 30bl** (Ralph F. Kresge)

Cover photograph reproduced with permission of Visuals Unlimited/Corbis

The publishers would like to thank Sue Glass for her assistance in the preparation of this book.

Every effort has been made to contact copyright holders of any material reproduced in this
book. Any omissions will be rectified in subsequent printings if notice is given to the publisher.

Disclaimer
All the Internet addresses (URLs) given in this book were valid at the time of going to press.
However, due to the dynamic nature of the Internet, some addresses may have changed, or
sites may have changed or ceased to exist since publication. While the author and publisher
regret any inconvenience this may cause readers, no responsibility for any such changes can
be accepted by either the author or the publisher.

 Some words are shown in bold, **like this.** You can
find the definitions for these words in the glossary.

Contents

Science Fair Basics

Starting a science fair project can be an exciting challenge. You can test a **scientific theory** by developing an appropriate scientific question. Then you can search, using the thoughtful steps of a well-planned experiment, for the answer to that question. It's like a treasure hunt of the mind.

In a way, your mission is to better understand how your world and the things in it work. You may be rewarded with a good grade or an award for your scientific hard work. But no matter what scores your project receives, you'll be a winner. That's because you will know a little bit more about your subject than you did before you started.

In this book, we'll look at nine science fair projects related to weather. We will discover how the Sun, air, water, and land work together to create rain, winds, clouds, lightning, and other aspects of weather.

Do Your Research

Is there something about weather and climate you've always wondered about? Something you don't quite understand but would like to? Then do a little research about the subject. Go to the library and check out books about the subject that interests you.

Use your favorite Internet search engine to find reliable online sources. Museums, universities, scientific journals, newspapers, and magazines are among the best sources for accurate research. Each experiment in this book lists some suggestions for further research.

When doing research you need to make sure your sources are reliable. Ask yourself the following questions about sources, especially those you find online.

Project Information

The Experiments

The beginning of each experiment contains a box like this.

Possible Question:

This question is a suggested starting point for your experiment. You will need to adapt the question to reflect your own interests.

Possible Hypothesis:

Don't worry if your hypothesis doesn't match the one listed here; this is only a suggestion.

Approximate Cost of Materials:

Discuss this with your parents before beginning work.

Materials Needed:

Make sure you can easily get all of the materials listed and gather them before beginning work.

Level of Difficulty:

There are three levels of experiments in this book: Easy, Intermediate, and Advanced. The level of difficulty is based on how long the experiment takes and how complicated it is.

1) How old is the source? Is it possible that the information is outdated?

2) Who wrote the source? Is there an identifiable author, and is the author qualified to write about the topic?

3) What is the purpose of the source? The website of a potato chip company is probably not the best place to look for information on healthful diets.

4) Is the information well documented? Can you tell where the author got his or her information?

Some websites allow you to "chat" online with experts. Make sure you discuss this with your parent or teacher before participating. Never give out private information, including your address or phone number, online.

Once you know a bit more about the subject you want to explore, you'll be ready to ask a science project question and form an intelligent **hypothesis.** A hypothesis is an educated guess about what the results of your experiment will be. Finally, you'll be ready to begin your science fair exploration!

Continued

A flash of lightning is one of the most dramatic events in nature. In this book, you'll learn how lightning and other weather events occur.

What Is an Experiment?

When you say you're going to "experiment," you may just mean that you're going to try something out. When a scientist uses that word, though, he or she means something else. In a proper experiment, you have **variables** and a **control.** A variable is something that changes. The independent variable is the thing you purposely change as part of the experiment. The dependent variable is the change that happens in response to the thing you do. The controlled variables, or control group, are the things you do not change so that you have something to compare your outcomes with. Here's an example: You want to test whether sunlight will heat up a container of water. You place three bowls of water in sunlight (Group A). You leave three identical bowls of water in a shady place indoors (Group B). The location of the bowls is the independent variable. The effect of sunlight on the water temperature is the dependent variable. Group B is the control group. To make sure your results are accurate, though, you need to do the experiment several times under the same conditions.

Some of the projects in this book are not proper experiments. They are projects designed to help you learn about a subject. You need to check with your teacher about whether these projects are appropriate for your science fair. Before beginning a project, make sure you know the rules about what kinds of projects and materials are allowed.

Your Hypothesis

Once you've decided what question you're going to try to answer, you'll want to make a scientific **prediction** of what you'll discover through your science project. For example, if you wonder whether the types of clouds you see in the sky have any effect on the weather, your question might be, "Do different types of clouds give clues about the weather?"

Remember, your hypothesis states the results you expect from your experiment. So your hypothesis in response to the above question might be, "The types of clouds we see give clues about the weather." Your research question also offers a good way to find out whether you can actually complete the steps needed for a successful project. If your question is, "How many raindrops fall during a thunderstorm?", it will be impossible to test your hypothesis, no matter how you express it. So, be sure the evidence to support your hypothesis is actually within reach.

Research Journal

It is very important to keep careful notes about your project. From start to finish, make entries in your research journal so you won't have to rely on memory when it comes time to create your display. What time did you start your experiment? How long did you work on it each day? What were the variables, or things that changed, about your experimental setting? How did they change and why? What things did you overlook in planning your project? How did you solve the problems, once you discovered them?

These are the kinds of questions you'll answer in your research journal. No detail is too small when it comes to scientific research. On pages 44–46 of this book, you'll find some tips on writing your report and preparing a winning display. Use these and the tips in each project as guides, but don't be afraid to get creative. Make your display, and your project, your own.

The Pressure Is On

Although you can't feel it, the weight of the air around us is constantly pressing down on Earth. This is called **air pressure.** It plays a key role in predicting weather: High pressure usually means cool, clear weather; low pressure can bring clouds, rain, even hurricanes (above). **Meteorologists,** scientists who study weather, use an instrument called a **barometer** to measure air pressure. Build a barometer of your own and start measuring weather the way the professionals do.

Do Your Research

This project involves making a barometer and using it to monitor changes in air pressure. Before you get started, do some research on air pressure systems and find out more about barometers and how they work. Then you can either make the barometer described in this project or come up with a design of your own.

Here are some books and websites you could start with in your research:

» Rodgers, Alan, and Angella Streluk. *Measuring the Weather: Wind and Air Pressure.* Chicago: Heinemann, 2007.

Project Information

Possible Question:

Can a homemade barometer accurately measure changes in air pressure?

Possible Hypothesis:

A homemade barometer will correctly show increases and decreases in air pressure.

Level of Difficulty:	Approximate Cost of Materials:
Intermediate	$10

Materials Needed:

» A balloon or strong plastic wrap
» Scissors
» Empty wide-mouthed jar, such as a mayonnaise or pickle jar
» Rubber band (optional)
» Drinking straw
» Tape
» Ruler
» Sheet of paper

» How a Barometer Measures Air Pressure
   http://www.usatoday.com/weather/wbaromtr.htm
» It's a Breeze: How Air Pressure Affects You
   http://kids.earth.nasa.gov/archive/air_pressure/index.html

Steps to Success:

1. Cut the balloon at its neck and throw the neck away. Stretch the balloon over the opening of the jar. The balloon should be tight like the cover of a drum. If you have trouble fitting the balloon over the jar yourself, have a helper hold the jar as you stretch the balloon over the jar's opening. Make sure the seal is tight—you don't want any air to escape from the jar. If necessary, secure the balloon in place with tape or a rubber band.

2. Tape one end of the straw to the middle of the "drum."

3. Use the ruler to mark lines ½ centimeter apart on the sheet of paper.

Continued

4. Tape the sheet of paper to a wall and position the barometer on a flat surface in front of it. Angle the barometer so the straw is close to the wall but not touching it.

5. Check the barometric reading for your area on a weather website. Write the reading next to the mark on the paper that is even with the top of the straw. Also record the reading in your research journal and make notes about the weather conditions at the time you took the reading.

6. Take readings twice a day. High pressure will cause the balloon on your barometer to be pushed in and the straw to rise slightly. Low pressure will cause the balloon to bulge out and the straw to point down (see illustration). Use the weather website to check your barometer's changes against those of the air pressure in your area. Record the actual readings along with the weather conditions in your journal.

7. Continue to take and record readings for one week.

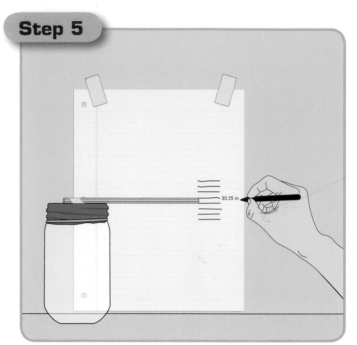

Step 5

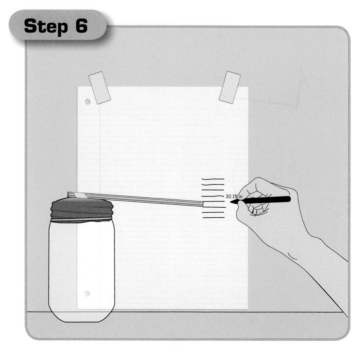

Step 6

Result Summary:

» Did the reading on your barometer change at each observation?

» Did you notice the top of your barometer bulging out or being pushed in at certain readings?

» How did the changes in your barometer compare with the air pressure readings you found online?

» What changes did you notice in the weather as your barometer rose and fell?

Added Activities to Give Your Project Extra Punch:

» Once you've tested your barometer for a few days, stop comparing your readings with those online. Continue to record the rise and fall of your barometer, and then make weather predictions based on your research.

» Do more research and make other weather instruments—you can build a whole weather station!

Display Extras:

» Research and present the history of the barometer.

» Display your homemade barometer along with photos of a real barometer.

» Research and report the historic high and low barometric pressure readings for your region.

The Warm and Cold of It

Heat from the Sun warms Earth's air, water, and land—but air, water, and land gain and lose heat at very different rates. This creates differences in temperature. Warm air rises and expands, and cooler air moves in to take its place. The result is wind. Temperature differences between land and sea can create everything from a pleasant sea breeze to a deadly hurricane. So which material loses heat the fastest? Find out with this "cool" project!

Do Your Research

This project explores how air, water, and land change temperatures at different rates. You will need to use a refrigerator, so be sure to get your parents' permission before you start. Begin by doing some research on the **heat capacity** of air, water, and land and the role it plays in the formation of wind, breezes, hurricanes, and other types of extreme weather. Once you've done some research, you can tackle this project or create your own version.

Here are some books and websites you could start with in your research:

» Cosgrove, Brian. *Eyewitness: Weather.* New York: Dorling Kindersley, 2004.
» Heat Capacity
   http://www.exploratorium.edu/climate/glossary/heat-capacity.html

Project Information

Possible Question:

Which loses heat the fastest—air, water, or soil?

Possible Hypothesis:

Air loses heat faster than both soil and water do.

Level of Difficulty:

Easy

Approximate Cost of Materials:

$12

Materials Needed:

» Three identical thermometers
» Three plastic cups
» Room-temperature water
» Potting soil or sand from a newly opened bag, enough to fill one plastic cup halfway
» Plate or tray large enough to hold three plastic cups
» Refrigerator

» Land and Sea Breeze Activity
http://www.carolina.com/earth/sea_breeze.asp
» Jetstream: An Online School for Weather: The Sea Breeze
http://www.srh.noaa.gov/jetstream/ocean/seabreezes.htm

Steps to Success:

1. Set up a data table in your research journal like the one shown below.

Step 1

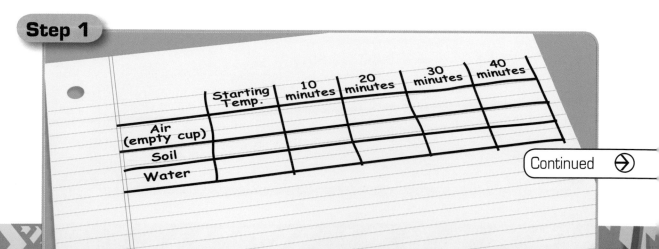

	Starting Temp.	10 minutes	20 minutes	30 minutes	40 minutes
Air (empty cup)					
Soil					
Water					

Continued →

2. Fill one cup about halfway with soil and another to the same level with water. Leave the third cup empty—it will hold only air.

3. Place one thermometer upright in each cup. Push the ball of the thermometer down into the soil. You will need to see enough of the thermometer in the soil to read the range between room and refrigerator temperature.

4. Allow enough time for the air, water, and soil to reach the same temperature.

5. Place all three cups on a plate or tray in the refrigerator.

Step 5

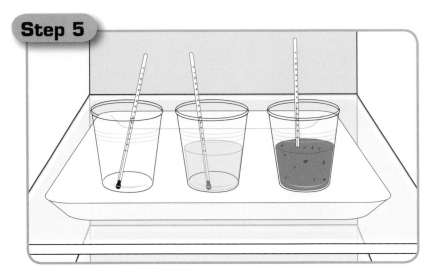

6. Read and record the cup temperatures at 10-minute intervals. Be sure to close the refrigerator door while waiting so you don't waste electricity.

7. Stop when the temperature in each of the three cups does not change for three straight readings.

Result Summary:

» Did the air, water, and soil change temperature at the same rate?

» If not, which material changed temperature the fastest?

» Which material changed temperature most slowly?

Added Activities to Give Your Project Extra Punch:

» Extend the experiment by removing the three cups from the refrigerator and placing them on a table or countertop at room temperature. Record the rate at which the temperature of the material in each cup increases.

» Using the same setup, place the cups under a desk lamp rather than in the refrigerator. Make sure each cup gets an equal amount of light. Take readings every five minutes to determine whether water, air, or soil absorbs heat the fastest. The lamp acts like the Sun heating Earth's oceans (the cup of water) and land (the cup of soil).

» Repeat the experiment using other materials, such as wet and dry clay. Use a wooden skewer or the sharp end of a compass to make a hole for the thermometer in two lumps of wet clay. Allow one lump to dry, and then place thermometers in both. Place both lumps on a tray in the refrigerator and compare the rate at which the temperature decreases in each.

» Use your knowledge of weather and your research data to explain how land and water temperature differences affect weather as wind moves from ocean to land.

Display Extras:

» Display your **data** using a color code, such as red to purple to blue, to represent the temperature change from warm to cold over the time interval you selected.

» Include an illustrated explanation of how hurricanes quickly lose energy after they leave the ocean and begin traveling over land.

» Display photographs taken from space that show the difference between ocean surface temperature and wind direction and the temperature and wind direction on land.

Moving Heat

The previous activity ("The Warm and Cold of It") showed that air, land, and water change temperature at different rates. The continuous rising of hot air and sinking of cooler air created by these temperature differences is called **convection.** This process also creates ocean currents, such as the Gulf Stream, which has a major effect on the climate of North America and Europe. (The Gulf Stream is shown above in red and orange along the East Coast of the United States.). In this project, you'll create a convection current using colored water in an aquarium.

Do Your Research

Convection is the transfer of heat through the movement of a liquid (such as water) or a gas (such as air). For this experiment, you'll use water to demonstrate how hot and cold fluids move in a convection current. Before beginning this project, do some research on convection to find out more about how this process affects weather. Then you can try this activity or come up with a version all your own.

Project Information

Possible Question:

What happens when both hot and cold water are added to a container of water?

Possible Hypothesis:

The hot water will rise to the top of the container, and the cold water will sink to the bottom.

Level of Difficulty:

Intermediate

Approximate Cost of Materials:

$15

Materials Needed:

» Room-temperature and hot water
» Freezer and ice cube tray
» Blue food coloring
» Small plastic aquarium or other clear container
» Red food coloring
» Bulb-type meat baster
» Clock or stopwatch

Here are some books and websites you could start with in your research:

» Davis, Barbara. *Weather and Climate*. Milwaukee: Gareth Stevens, 2007.
» NASA: For Kids Only: Earth Science Enterprise
   http://kids.earth.nasa.gov/facts.htm
» Convection: http://encyclopedia.kids.net.au/page/co/Convection
» Jetstream: An Online School for Weather: The Transfer of Heat Energy
   http://www.srh.weather.gov/srh/jetstream/atmos/heat.htm

Steps to Success:

1. The night before you do this project, fill an ice cube tray with water and add a few drops of blue food coloring to two or three of the cubes. (You'll need only one ice cube for the experiment, but it's a good idea to make extras.)

Continued

2. Fill the aquarium or other container three-quarters full with room-temperature water.

3. Mix a few drops of red food coloring into a cup of hot water.

4. Carefully fill the meat baster with the hot red water.

5. Drop a blue ice cube into one end of the aquarium.

6. Insert the meat baster into the aquarium on the side opposite the ice cube. Put the tip of the baster as close to the bottom of the aquarium as possible and squirt a small amount of red water into the tank.

Step 6

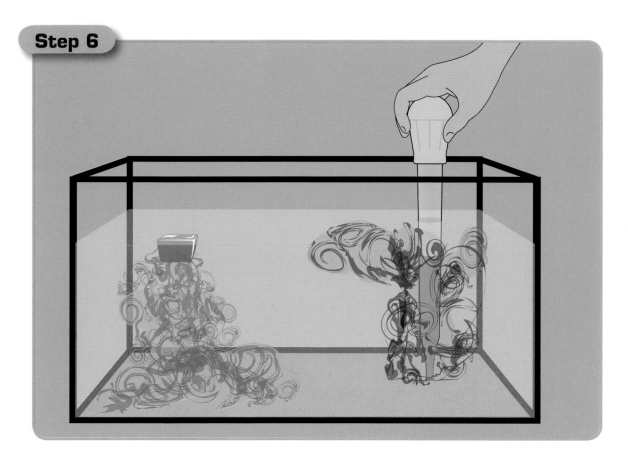

7. Observe and record the movement of the water until it stops moving and the colors are blended. This will take a few minutes.

Result Summary:

» Did the warm water rise to the top of the aquarium? If so, how long did that take?

» Did the ice melt and sink to the bottom of the aquarium? If so, how long did that take?

» How long did it take the colors to mix completely?

Added Activities to Give Your Project Extra Punch:

» Expand the project by clamping a small aquarium heater to one end of your aquarium. Use two clothespins to clamp a soft ice pack at the other end. Then follow steps 2–6 from the project. Observe how the water moves around the aquarium.

» Take photos of the rising and falling of the colored hot and cold water in your aquarium. Include the photos in your display.

Display Extras:

» Display pictures or illustrations with arrows that show convection currents in action, such as steam rising from a bowl of soup.

» Demonstrate the activity at your science fair station.

» Include a diagram that explains how convection currents act as a conveyor belt that affects weather and climate in your region by moving hot and cold masses of air and water.

It's Raining Indoors

How is it possible that rivers constantly flow into oceans and inches and inches of rain falls each year, yet the land isn't completely covered with water? All of the water on Earth and in the **atmosphere** is constantly recycled through the **water cycle**—a process that is vital for the survival of all living things. In this project, you'll use only a few household items to re-create the water cycle.

Do Your Research

This project deals with the water cycle—the process by which water goes from a solid or liquid to water vapor and back again. Before you start, do some research to find out more about the key parts of the water cycle: **evaporation, condensation, precipitation,** and **collection.** Then see the water cycle in action using this project or a similar project you design yourself.

Here are some books and websites where you can begin your research:

» O'Hare, Ted. *Studying Weather.* Vero Beach, Fla.: Rourke Publishing, 2003.

» Trueit, Trudi Strain. *The Water Cycle.* New York: Franklin Watts, 2002.

» Animated Diagram of the Water Cycle
   http://www.bbc.co.uk/schools/riversandcoasts/water_cycle/rivers/index.shtml

Project Information

Possible Question:

Can "rain" be made indoors?

Possible Hypothesis:

Rain can be made indoors by placing a sealed bag of ice over a container of hot water.

Level of Difficulty:

Easy

Approximate Cost of Materials:

$0

Materials Needed:

» Tall clear pitcher or another clear container, such as an empty 2-liter soda bottle cut at the shoulder
» Hot water
» Large resealable plastic bag filled with ice
» Clock or watch

» The Water Cycle: http://www.kidzone.ws/water/
» Water Science for Schools: The Water Cycle http://ga.water.usgs.gov/edu/watercycle.html

Steps to Success:

1. Carefully fill the container about one-quarter full with hot water.

2. Place the sealed ice-filled plastic bag on top of the pitcher, making sure the opening is completely covered. The sides of the container should fog up a bit almost immediately. Place the ice-covered pitcher in direct sunlight.

3. Record how long it takes for droplets of water (condensation) to form on the bottom of the bag. This will take a few minutes.

Continued

Step 3

4. Record how long it takes before the droplets start to fall into the container.

5. Continue to observe the container for 10 minutes after the first droplet falls. Count the total number of droplets that fall into the container.

6. Repeat the experiment at least two times and compare the results from each test.

The Water Cycle

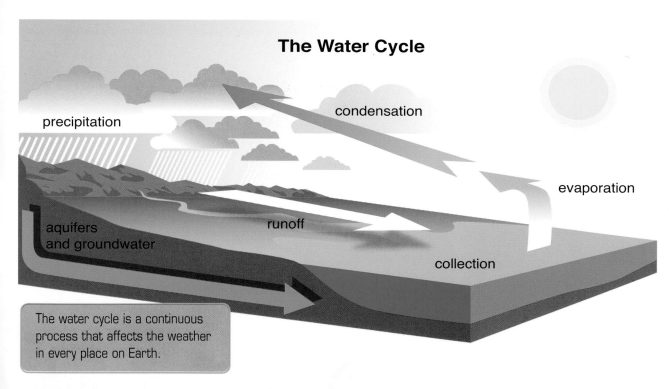

precipitation

condensation

evaporation

aquifers and groundwater

runoff

collection

The water cycle is a continuous process that affects the weather in every place on Earth.

Result Summary:

» How long did it take for droplets to form on the bottom of the ice-filled bag?

» How long did it take before the droplets increased in size and then fell like rain?

» Did each test produce the same results? If not, what variables might have affected the results?

Added Activities to Give Your Project Extra Punch:

» Repeat the project using more, and then less, hot water in the container. Does this affect the amount of time it takes for condensation to appear?

» Add food coloring to the water to test whether the water droplets will be colored or clear.

» Add salt to the water and taste whether the water droplets that form on the bag are salty or fresh.

» Research which areas of the world get the most and least rainfall. Use your knowledge of the water cycle to explain why.

Display Extras:

» Re-create the project. (You will need an insulated bottle filled with hot water at your station.) Have a magnifying glass on hand for close observation of the water droplets as they form.

» Display rain photographs and a poster illustrating the water cycle.

Cloud in a Container

Many clouds *look* like they're made of big, fluffy cotton balls. But anyone who has ever walked through fog knows that it *feels* like it's made mostly of wet, cold air. This project will show you how to make your own cloud in a matter of a few minutes.

Do Your Research

For this project, you'll create a cloud using a similar setup to the one used in the previous project ("It's Raining Indoors"). You'll need a lighted match to make the experiment work, so ask an adult to help you. Before you begin, research clouds and how they form. Then you can either try this activity or put your own unique spin on it.

Here are some books and websites you could start with in your research:

» Rodgers, Alan, and Angella Streluk. *Measuring the Weather: Cloud Cover.* Chicago: Heinemann, 2007.

» NASA Space Place: Let's Find Out More About Clouds! http://spaceplace.jpl.nasa.gov/en/kids/cloudsat_puz3.shtml

Project Information

Possible Question:

Is it possible to make a cloud?

Possible Hypothesis:

Clouds can be made using a few simple materials.

Level of Difficulty:

Intermediate

Approximate Cost of Materials:

$0

Materials Needed:

» Tall clear pitcher or another clear container, such as an empty 2-liter soda bottle cut at the shoulder
» Hot water
» Large resealable plastic bag filled with ice
» Match
» Sheet of black construction paper
» Clock or watch
» Tape (optional)
» Adult supervisor

» How Do Clouds Form? http://ksnn.larc.nasa.gov/k2/s_cloudsForm.html
» Fog & Mist: What Is Fog? http://library.thinkquest.org/C003603/english/fogandmist/whatisfog.shtml

Steps to Success:

1. Carefully fill the container about one-quarter full with hot water.

2. Place the sealed ice-filled plastic bag on top of the container, making sure the opening is completely covered. The sides of the container should fog up a bit almost immediately.

3. Record how long it takes for droplets of water to form on the bottom of the bag. This will take a few minutes.

4. Once water droplets begin to form on the bottom of the bag of ice, have your adult helper light the match and then blow it out.

ADULT SUPERVISION REQUIRED

Continued

5. Quickly lift the bag of ice from the top of the container and drop the still-smoking match into the container.

6. Replace the bag of ice immediately.

7. Hold the construction paper behind the container, or tape it to a wall behind the container. This will allow you to see the cloud more clearly. Record how long it takes for the container to start to get cloudy.

8. Remove the bag of ice to allow the cloud to escape from the container. Note how the cloud feels on your hands and face.

9. Repeat the experiment at least two times and compare the results from each test.

Step 7

Result Summary:

» How long did it take for a cloud to form?

» What did the cloud feel like?

» How long did it take for the cloud to disappear?

» Did each test produce the same results? If not, what variables might have affected the results?

Added Activities to Give Your Project Extra Punch:

» Add red or blue food coloring to the water and see whether it creates a colored cloud.

» For a different view of your cloud, try the activity in a darkened room and shine a flashlight on the container.

» Research and report on cloud seeding and how it is used to create rain.

Display Extras:

» Include photographs of clouds and fog.

» Decorate your display with model clouds created with cotton balls or packing materials.

Sky Watch

You've probably seen all types of shapes in clouds—an elephant, a castle, maybe even your favorite cartoon character. But did you know that you're also seeing clues about what the weather will be later? Cumulus clouds are known as "fair-weather clouds". Other types, such as nimbus clouds, bring rain or snow. If you'd like to predict the weather by watching the clouds, this project will show you how.

Do Your Research

For this project, you will observe the types of clouds in the sky and note the weather that follows. Give yourself plenty of time. You'll want to observe a few different cloud types and different weather conditions. Before you start, do some research on the different types of clouds. Then you can tackle this project. Or, you may come up with your own unique project after you've learned more.

Here are some books and websites that can help you get started:

» Locker, Thomas. *Cloud Dance.* New York: Voyager, 2003.
» S'COOL: On-Line Cloud Chart
  http://asd-www.larc.nasa.gov/SCOOL/cldchart.html
» Jetstream: An Online School for Weather: Clouds
  http://www.srh.noaa.gov/jetstream/synoptic/clouds.htm
» BBC Weather: Types of Clouds
  http://www.bbc.co.uk/weather/features/weatherbasics/cloud_types.shtml

Project Information

Possible Question:

Can you predict the weather by observing clouds?

Possible Hypothesis:

Clouds can tell us what type of weather to expect.

Materials Needed:

» A cloud chart (can be found online at sites such as http://asd-www.larc.nasa.gov/SCOOL/cldchart.html)

Level of Difficulty:

Easy

Approximate Cost of Materials:

$0

Steps to Success:

1. For each day that you plan to observe the sky, write the date at the top of a blank page in your research journal.

2. Divide each page into two sections—one for observations made in the morning and the other for observations in the afternoon.

Step 3

Date: September 20

Morning

Cloud type(s): Stratus
Cloud cover: 100%; completely cloudy
Weather conditions: Cool, no wind
Prediction: cloudy skies, maybe some rain

Afternoon

Cloud type(s):
Cloud cover:
Weather conditions:
Prediction:

3. Add the following headings to both sections on the page: cloud types; **cloud cover**—the amount of the sky that is covered with clouds; weather conditions (hot, cold, sunny, raining, etc.); and your prediction for what the weather will be later in the day or the next day.

Continued

4. Observe the sky every morning. Compare the clouds in the sky with those on your cloud chart. You may see more than one type of cloud at a time. In your research journal, record the types of clouds you see and the cloud cover. Also record the weather and your prediction for the weather at your next observation. Follow the same procedure each afternoon.

5. Continue your observations for at least two weeks. You should observe each type of cloud, and the weather that follows it, more than once.

When you see cumulonimbus clouds, you can expect rain and thunder in the near future.

These are not pieces of cotton—they're cumulus clouds. These clouds are sometimes called "fair-weather clouds".

Is it a gray day? Low-lying stratus clouds are probably to blame. They often cover the entire sky.

High, wispy cirrus clouds are signs of pleasant weather. But expect a change in weather if they start to thicken.

Result Summary:

» Which types of clouds did you see most often?
» Did you correctly predict the weather conditions that followed each observation?
» Did you notice different types of clouds in the sky at the same time? If so, how did this seem to affect the type of weather that followed?

Added Activities to Give Your Project Extra Punch:

» Take photographs of the sky during each observation.
» Research the Latin root words for the name of each cloud type. Explain how the Latin meanings give clues about what each type of cloud looks like.

Display Extras:

» Create a chart or graph that illustrates the number of days you saw each type of cloud. Include photos of the various cloud types you observed.
» Use cotton balls to make a 3-D cloud chart.

Lightning Strikes

Lightning is definitely one of Mother Nature's coolest tricks—an all-natural fireworks display. Want to see some sparks fly? You can duplicate the conditions necessary to produce sparks of lightning right in your own home.

Do Your Research

For this project, you will build an **electrophorus**—a device that produces static electricity. You will find that it works best indoors during cold, dry weather and that it won't work at all if the weather is hot and humid. Before you get started, do some research on static electricity and how lightning is produced. Then you can either build this electrophorus or create your own static electricity generator.

Here are some books and websites that will help with your research:

» Simon, Seymour. *Lightning.* New York: William Morrow, 2006.

» What Causes a Lightning Flash?
http://ksnn.larc.nasa.gov/webtext.cfm?unit=lightning

» Everyday Mysteries: Fun Science Facts from the Library of Congress
http://www.loc.gov/rr/scitech/mysteries/static.html

Project Information

Possible Question:

What materials will create static electricity?

Possible Hypothesis:

Wool and other fabrics will create static electricity.

Level of Difficulty:

Intermediate

Approximate Cost of Materials:

$2

Materials Needed:

» Thumbtack
» Disposable aluminum pie plate
» Pencil with an eraser
» Wool sock or mitten, or a scrap of wool fabric
» Styrofoam plate or a small block of Styrofoam
» Scrap of leather (available at a fabric store)
» Lightbulb

Steps to Success:

1. Push the thumbtack through the center of the aluminum pie plate.

Step 2

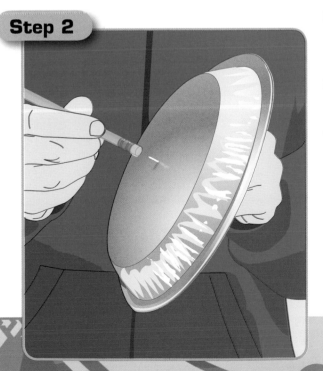

2. Push the eraser end of the pencil onto the thumbtack to create a handle.

3. Rub the sock or mitten quickly back and forth over the Styrofoam.

4. Pick up the pie plate by its handle and place it upside down on top of the Styrofoam. The pie plate and Styrofoam should stick together. You have just created an electrophorus.

Continued

5. Turn off the lights in the room and carefully touch your finger to the pie plate. You should see a spark and feel a little shock.

Step 5

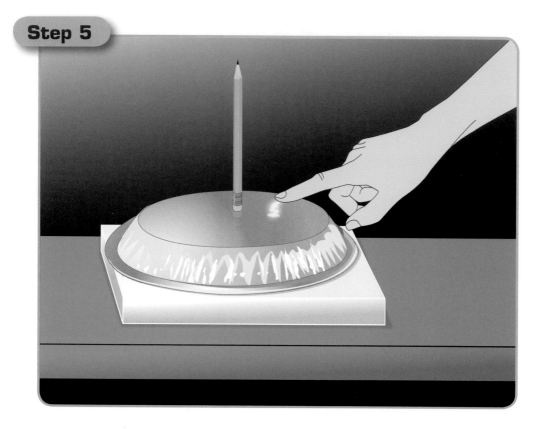

6. Rate the shock and the spark on a scale of 1 (small) to 5 (large) in your research journal.

7. Repeat step 3, this time with the scrap of leather, and then repeat steps 4–6.

8. Repeat the test by rubbing the glass end of a lightbulb over the Styrofoam. Finally, test whether you get a shock after rubbing the Styrofoam against your hair. Compare the shock and sparks generated by each object.

9. Repeat the experiment on each of the next two days. Compare the shock and sparks generated by each object on the different days.

Result Summary:

» Which material produced the biggest shock?

» Which material produced the biggest spark?

» Did any materials fail to produce a shock and spark? If so, why might that be?

» Were the results the same on different days? If not, what variables might have been involved?

Added Activities to Give Your Project Extra Punch:

» Re-create your experiment at the science fair and invite the judges to give it a try.

» Research and explain why this experiment will not work in hot, humid weather.

» Research Benjamin Franklin and other early scientists who studied electricity.

» After charging the electrophorus (step 4), bring a small fluorescent tube (like the ones used in camping lanterns) near the aluminum plate. Touch one terminal of the tube with your finger and touch the terminal at the other end to the charged plate. The tube should briefly glow.

Display Extras:

» Include your electrophorus in your display.

» Decorate your board with some dramatic photos of lightning.

» Display the various materials you used in your project.

Weather Wise

Long before there were TV meteorologists, sailors, farmers, and other people who worked outdoors made weather predictions based on their experiences. Then they made up easy-to-remember sayings, or proverbs, about what they observed. How accurate are these sayings? You be the judge!

Do Your Research

This project involves testing the accuracy of weather sayings, such as "Clear Moon, frost soon." Research weather sayings and the science behind them, and then pick one or two that you think you will be able to test. Keep in mind the time of the year and the type of weather in your region. (For example, if it's spring, don't pick a saying that deals with snow.) Plan to make daily observations for about a month. This should allow you to see many types of weather changes. Once you've read about popular sayings and what they mean, you can tackle this project or come up with one of your own.

Here are some books and websites you could start with in your research:

» *The Old Farmer's Almanac.* Dublin, N.H.: Yankee Publishing, 1792–present.
» Everyday Mysteries: Fun Science Facts from the Library of Congress
   http://www.loc.gov/rr/scitech/mysteries/weather-sailor.html

Project Information

Possible Question:

Do folk sayings provide useful advice about future weather events?

Materials Needed:

» Binder for collecting weather reports

Possible Hypothesis:

Yes, some folk sayings do provide useful advice about future weather events.

Level of Difficulty:

Intermediate

Approximate Cost of Materials:

$0

» Weather Sayings
http://www.metoffice.gov.uk/education/primary/students/sayings.html
» American Folklore: Rain Proverbs and Sayings
http://www.americanfolklore.net/folktales/rain-lore.html

Possible Sayings to Test

- Ring around the Moon, rain or snow will come soon.

- Red sky at night, sailor's delight. Red sky in morning, sailors take warning.

- When grass is dry at morning light, look for rain before the night.

- Rain before seven, fine by eleven.

- Thunder in the morning, all day storming. Thunder at night is the traveler's delight.

- No weather is ill if the wind be still.

Steps to Success:

1. Choose weather sayings that are appropriate to your area and the time of year. To increase your odds of seeing something, select more than one weather proverb to investigate. Weather patterns are different all over the world, so the weather described in some proverbs may not occur in your area. Many sayings are related to rain or other forms of precipitation—test these sayings during a month in which a few rainstorms are expected.

Continued

2. Research the science behind your selected sayings, using resources such as those included in Do Your Research. The saying investigated here is "Ring around the Moon, rain or snow will come soon." Testing this saying requires some research into the phases of the Moon.

3. Check the weather forecast in your local newspaper or online. Save the daily weather forecast in your binder.

4. Observe the sky at the same time each night. Note what you see in a chart in your research journal, even if you don't see a ring around the Moon. Note the phases of the Moon and if any part of the Moon is covered by clouds. Also record the weather conditions.

Step 4

Date: September 20

Morning weather: Cool, clear skies
Evening weather: Colder, clear skies
Phase of the Moon: First quarter
Ring around the Moon? No
Description of ring: N/A

5. Observe the weather the next morning and note the weather conditions in your research journal. If it's raining, note whether it's a drizzle, heavy rain, a steady rain all day, and so on.

6. Repeat steps 3–5 each night for a month.

7. On nights you observe a ring around the Moon, draw a picture of what you see in your research journal. Note how clearly you can see the ring and how thick it appears to be.

Result Summary:

» On how many nights did you see a ring around the Moon?

» Each time, did rain or snow follow the next day?

» Did you see any relationship between the thickness of the ring and the amount of rainfall or snowfall the next day?

» If you didn't see a ring around the Moon on any night, why might that be?

» Did it rain or snow on any days after you didn't see a ring around the Moon?

Added Activities to Give Your Project Extra Punch:

» Take photos of the Moon on the nights that a ring appears. Create a chart that shows the level of rainfall on each of the days that follow.

» Based on your observations, try to come up with your own weather-related saying.

Display Extras:

» Display the binder that holds each day's weather forecasts.

» Create a poster that includes other well-known weather sayings alongside photos that show those weather events.

» Dress as a sailor, a farmer, or another person who might use these sayings. Explain how the sayings are important to that person's work.

Moonlight reflected from ice crystals high in Earth's atmosphere creates a ring around the Moon.

What's Cooking?

You've probably heard people say it's hot enough outside to fry an egg—but is there any truth to the saying? Does the Sun actually produce enough heat to cook food? This project will help you find out!

Do Your Research

For the best results, try this project on a warm sunny day between the hours of 10 A.M. and 2 P.M. Remember to wear sunscreen and never look directly at the Sun. A solar oven can get very hot, so make sure an adult is present when you perform the project. Before you begin, do some research on the many ways in which the Sun affects weather. You'll also want to learn about solar energy and solar cookers. Then you'll be ready to try this project or come up with one of your own.

Here are some books and websites you could start with in your research:

» Cosgrove, Brian. *Eyewitness: Weather.* New York: Dorling Kindersley, 2004.
» Sun's Heat Powers Weather
http://www.usatoday.com/weather/tg/wglobale/wglobale.htm
» Energy Kid's Page: Solar Energy
http://www.eia.doe.gov/kids/energyfacts/sources/renewable/solar.html

Project Information

Possible Question:

Can heat from the Sun's rays be used to cook food?

Possible Hypothesis:

Food can be cooked by trapping heat from the Sun's rays in a solar oven.

Level of Difficulty:

Advanced

Approximate Cost of Materials:

$10

Materials Needed:

» Empty pizza box
» Scissors
» Aluminum foil
» Glue
» Plastic oven bag
» Masking tape or duct tape
» Ingredients to make a s'more: two graham crackers, a chocolate bar, and marshmallows
» Oven thermometer
» Pencil or wooden skewer (optional)
» Spatula
» Oven mitts
» Adult supervisor

A s'more is made of melted chocolate and marshmallows sandwiched between two graham crackers.

Steps to Success:

1. Draw a large square on the top of the pizza box, leaving a 1-inch (2.5-centimeter) border all around.

2. Cut along three sides of the square, leaving the line at the back of the box uncut.

ADULT SUPERVISION REQUIRED

3. Gently fold the cut cardboard top back at the uncut line to create a flap.

Continued ⮕

4. Cut a piece of aluminum foil to the size of the underside of the flap. Glue the foil in place, smoothing out any wrinkles.

5. Make a "window" in the pizza box by cutting a piece of the oven bag slightly larger than the hole in the top of the box. Tape the plastic in place on the underside of the hole. Be sure there are no gaps between the plastic and the sides of the box so heat can't escape.

Step 5

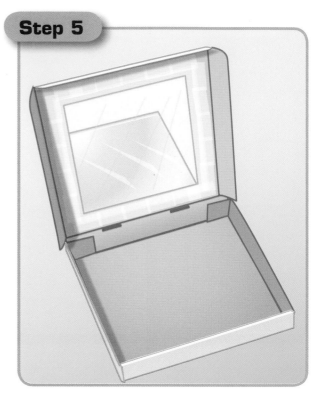

6. Cut another piece of aluminum foil to the size of the inside of the pizza box. Glue it in place, smoothing out any wrinkles.

7. Place the s'more and the oven thermometer on the foil in the box. Close the window.

8. Position the oven to face the Sun. Make sure the aluminum-covered flap is folded back far enough to reflect the maximum amount of sunlight directly into the box. Prop the flap open with a pencil or skewer if necessary. Remember not to look directly at the Sun.

Step 8

9. Look through the window to take temperature readings and observe the s'more every 10 minutes.

10. Once the chocolate is melted, use the spatula to remove the s'more. The oven will be hot, so be sure to wear oven mitts.

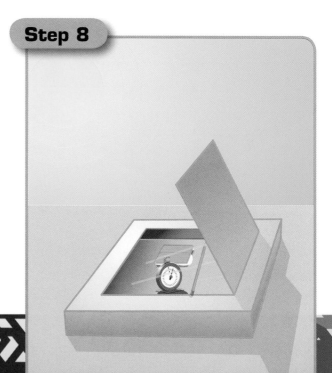

Result Summary:

» What was the maximum temperature the oven reached?
» How long did it take to reach the maximum temperature?
» How long did it take for the chocolate to melt?
» At what temperature did the chocolate melt?

Added Activities to Give Your Project Extra Punch:

» Demonstrate how to make a solar cooker and provide a pattern and directions so that other students can make one at home.

» Try other dishes in your solar oven, such as English muffin pizzas. Record how long it takes for the cheese to melt and the muffins to get crispy. **Do not use foods that can cause illness if undercooked, such as eggs and meats.**

» Note the air temperature at the time you started the project and at 10-minute intervals as the oven heats up. Create a line graph that compares the increase and decrease of the oven and air temperatures over the course of the project.

Display Extras:

» Include the solar oven in your display.
» Create a chart that compares the pros and cons of cooking with a solar oven.
» Include photos of the s'more before and after it cooked in your solar oven.

The Competition

Learning is its own reward, but winning the science fair is pretty fun, too. Here are some things to keep in mind if you want to do well in the competition:

1) Creativity counts. Do not simply copy an experiment from this or any other book. You need to change the experiment so that it is uniquely your own.

2) You will need to be able to explain your project to the judges. Being able to talk intelligently about your work will reassure the judges that you learned something and that you did the work yourself. You may have to repeat the same information to different judges, so make sure you've practiced it ahead of time. You will also need to be able to answer the judges' questions about your methods and results.

3) You will need to present your materials in an appealing manner. Discuss with your teacher whether or not it is acceptable to have someone help you with artistic flourishes to your display.

Keep these guidelines in mind for your display:

» Type and print: Display the project title, the question, the hypothesis, and the collected **data** in clean, neatly crafted paper printouts that you can mount on a sturdy poster display.

» Visibility: Be sure to print your title and headings in large type and in energetic colors. If your project is about the Sun, you might use bright reds, oranges, and yellows to bring your letters to life. If your project is about plant life, you might use greens and browns to capture an earthy mood. You want your project to be easily visible in a crowd of other projects.

» Standing display: Be sure your display can stand on its own. Office supply stores have thick single-, double-, and triple-section display boards available in several sizes and colors that will work nicely as the canvas for your science fair masterpiece. Mount your core data—your discoveries—on this display, along with photos and other relevant materials (charts, resource articles, interviews, etc.).

» Attire: Dress neatly and comfortably for the fair. You may be standing on your feet for a long time.

4) The final report is an important part of your project.
   Make sure the following things are in your final report:

» **Title page:** the first page of your report, with your name and the name of your project (similar to the first page of this book)

» **Table of contents:** a list of what's included in your report (similar to page 3 of this book)

» **Research:** the research you did that led you to choose this topic and helped you formulate your question

» **Your project question:** what you tested

» **Your hypothesis:** your prediction of how your experiment would answer the question

» **Materials:** the things you used to conduct your experiment

» **Methods:** the steps you took to perform your experiment

» **Observations:** some of the data you recorded in your research journal

» **Conclusion:** how closely your hypothesis lined up with the results

» **Bibliography:** books, articles, and other resources you used in researching and preparing your project. Discuss with your teacher the appropriate way to list your sources.

» **Acknowledgments:** recognition of those who helped you prepare and work on your project

Prepare to be Judged

Each science fair is different, but you will probably be assigned points based on your performance in each of the categories below. Make sure to talk to your teacher about how your specific science fair will be judged. Ask yourself the questions in each category to see whether you've done the best possible job.

Your objectives
» Did you present original, creative ideas?
» Did you state the problem or question clearly?
» Did you define the variables and use controls?
» Did you relate your research to the problem or question?

Your skills
» Do you understand your results?
» Did you do your own work? It's OK for an adult to help you for safety reasons, but not to do the work for you. If you cannot explain the experiment, the equipment, and the steps you took, the judges may not believe that you did your own work.

Data collection and interpretation
» Did you keep a research journal?
» Was your experiment planned correctly to collect the data you needed?
» Did you correctly interpret your results?
» Could someone else repeat the experiment by reading your report?
» Are your conclusions based only on the results of your experiment?

Presentation
» Is your display attractive and complete?
» Do you have a complete report?
» Did you use reliable sources and document them correctly?
» Can you answer questions about your work?

Glossary

air pressure force caused by the weight of air pressing down on a given point on Earth; also called atmospheric pressure or barometric pressure

atmosphere layer of gases that surrounds Earth

barometer instrument that measures air pressure

cloud cover amount of the sky that is covered by clouds

collection stage of the water cycle in which precipitation builds up in oceans, lakes, streams, and other bodies of water

condensation process in which water vapor changes to a liquid

control sample in an experiment that is left unchanged and used for comparison with other samples that have variables

convection transfer of heat caused by circular movement of air or water

data factual information

electrophorus device that collects and discharges static electricity

evaporation process in which water changes from a liquid to a vapor or gas

heat capacity amount of heat needed to increase the temperature of a substance by one degree Celsius

hypothesis informed guess based on information at hand

meteorologist scientist who studies and predicts weather

precipitation process in which water (in the form of rain, hail, sleet, or snow) falls from clouds to Earth

prediction say in advance what you think will happen, based on scientific study

scientific theory belief based on tested evidence and facts

variable something that can change; is not set or fixed

water cycle continuous cycle in which water moves from Earth to the atmosphere and back again

Index